Girl,

FORGET ALL THAT!

MOVING FORWARD AFTER A RELATIONSHIP ENDS

PART 1

Disclaimer

All the material in this book is provided for educational and informational purposes only. No responsibility can be taken for any results or outcomes resulting from using this material.

While every attempt has been made to provide information that is both accurate and effective, the author assumes no responsibility for the accuracy or use/misuse of this information.

Dedication

For every woman that has felt alone
or lost in her journey after a relationship ends

Acknowledgments

Writing a book is a challenge already, so writing a book about something so painful and personal made it an even bigger challenge. There is a quote that could not have been more relevant to my process in writing this book. It is "Teamwork makes the dream work." God knew I needed a dynamic group of people to help me carry out this assignment He gave me. To the V.I.P^2 Business Connections and Networking Group of Keystone Business Institute, you guys are unbelievable! Thank you so much for helping me form the right questions based on my vision for the book. My accountability partner for being an excellent proofreader with such sound advice and support! Keandra Ward of Keystone Business Institute, thank you for hosting the book challenge so that I have the information to write, publish, and market this book effectively. You all are amazing beyond words. There would definitely not be a book without the anonymous survey participants who may not read this book but thank you for being genuine and thorough about your feelings after the breakup and healing process so that other women can be free. I also have to thank God for giving me the courage to write this book.

Table of Contents

Intro

I didn't want to write about my recent breakup because I didn't want to relive it, but I knew God wanted me to use my story to help others. My company, Breaking it Down with C Jackson is all about being transparent about sex, the good, bad, and ugly. So, I had to be honest about what happened to a relationship I mentioned in my first book, on social media, and at events I hosted. I wanted women to know how I handled a broken relationship that was very public and that would possibly lead to marriage. After my breakup, I felt alone and like people wanted me to just move on. What I really needed was for more women to share their feelings and experiences after a breakup. As I was looking for books on how to heal from breakups for Christians, I didn't find a lot, so I decided I would write my own. I wanted to create an honest and open conversation about healing from a breakup. Satan loves for us to be miserable, and if we keep this information a secret, others won't be free and live the abundant life God wants us to live. Breakups can suck, but they happen, and our hearts must be healed so that our lives won't become miserable. According to Proverbs 4:23, the issues of life flow out of our hearts so we must guard it. In addition, Proverbs 14:30 states that a calm and undisturbed mind and heart are the life and health of the body, but envy, jealousy, and wrath are like a rottenness of the bones. So, it is important to heal a broken heart. *Girl, Forget All That!* is not a man bash or self-pity book, but it is a book to help women properly move on after a difficult breakup and discover or rediscover the woman God created them to be. I am not the only one that has experienced a difficult breakup, so I want to share with you the stories of nine women including mine about our most difficult breakup and how we moved forward.

Isaiah 43:18-19

New Living Translation (NLT)

[18] "But forget all that— it is nothing
compared to what I am going to do.
[19] For I am about to do something new.
See, I have already begun!
Do you not see it? I will make
a pathway through the wilderness.
I will create rivers in the
dry wasteland.

Chapter 1

My Moment of Truth

In June 2018, I was ready to take on the Washington DC/Maryland area with my last boyfriend to see if this relationship would actually lead to marriage. I was finally ready to move to be closer to him but what he told me on June 5, 2018, changed all of MY plans. Before I get to how our relationship ended, let's look at the beginning of our relationship. In 2011, while I was being trained to be a singles mentor at my church, I was introduced to my ex as someone who I thought had a crush on me. One of the most important things I had learned about him was that he was a virgin and was waiting until marriage to have sex. I thought, *"WOW! Are you serious? A male virgin in his 30s? I HAVE to meet him!"* Well, it turned out he wasn't interested in me, but our mutual friend wanted us to connect. We talked at a singles' ministry event for two minutes, and then he went off to talk to someone else. I didn't see him again until about two months later. He had a girlfriend with him at church. I found out much later that he was casually dating her when our friend tried to hook us up. *Bummer.* But what happened 2 1/2 years later caught me totally by surprise! I was asked what I had thought about him from *another* woman at my church. I couldn't believe it. This guy had moved to a different state, yet here was someone **else** trying to hook us up! Well, she gave him my number, he called, and we talked on the phone for two hours the first night! We started dating from there on. It was amazing to have a boyfriend actually willing to wait with me. I felt like I had hit the ***JACKPOT***! He had a deep relationship with God, so that helped him treat me well and wait for sex until marriage. Within the first 3 months of our relationship, my ex had decided that I was the one and he was preparing for marriage, but I was not sure. I had called off our relationship within the first five months of dating due to him being very critical of me and strict, but I just knew there was something else to this relationship, so I stayed. As a result, I got to experience a lot of positive things, and I grew so much because of it. I absolutely loved that he was a good listener. I learned how to persevere better. I loved the gifts he would give me because the gifts I loved the most had eternal value such as books for my business or my spiritual walk. He was also a huge asset to writing my first book and my celibacy journey. My spiritual walk was also developed because of his recommendations of teachers from whom I still receive wisdom today. He was also good at not taking offense easily, but I was offended easily. And I saved this for last. I'm a pretty small person and I like my men to be a little buff, so he had the physique I was looking for lol. So that was a bonus. I saw myself grow so much from this relationship. I learned to be more selfless, I learned how to speak another love language (one of his love languages was not one I was used to expressing), I learned to be more supportive, understand the roles of a wife, walk in the God type of love, handle criticism better, and learn not to take things personally but to understand a person's personality, background, and/or communication style before I took offense at something they said or did. We talked about marriage a lot for the first two years of the relationship, but in the latter part, discussing marriage came more from me.

Maintaining this long-distance relationship became challenging, especially in 2016. I felt something change about him. He became less affectionate and emotionally distant. He no longer made a big deal about seeing me in person. I felt unwanted and unloved. I asked him about it several times, but he didn't tell me the truth. Instead, he would apologize and make a few attempts to fix the problem or make it seem like I was angry for no reason, but nothing really changed. In Fall 2017, I asked about his plans for the next year and he didn't mention me. He brought up the fact that in the past I said I wanted to be in Memphis for a minute. This was true, but I was ready to move now. I then told him I would not date him for another four years. The relationship should have ended then, but I ignored all the red flags again. I continued making plans to move near him because I wanted to see where this relationship would go once we were in the same city. I tried so hard to fix our relationship by continuing to suggest long-distance dating ideas and reading books related to dating and marriage. I continued to express my love for him, but NOTHING worked. As my love for him grew stronger, his love for me seemed to lessen. The last time I saw him was Christmas 2017. Everything went fine for most of the time

I was there. We even went around looking at homes together. The last day we were together was sad because he said something that made me feel like I was not good enough for him, and I went to the bathroom to cry for a couple of minutes. Eventually, I tried to get past this feeling but later when I got to the airport, I told him that I know that I am a good woman, to which he agreed, but I was not going to wait on him forever and I walked into the airport, left and went home. That was the last thing I had said to him in person. Later that night I sent him an email telling him why I was a good woman and I gave him the opportunity to leave the relationship if I was not good enough for him. When I talked to him on the phone the next day, I gave him an ultimatum, something I never wanted to do. I told him either I move there, or this relationship is over. He still didn't leave the relationship, so I continued preparing to move. I asked God to stop the move if it wasn't His will because I was determined to do it my way despite the doubts I was having.

On June 3, I finally got tired of the way he was acting about the move. After I got no answer when I called him, I recorded a message asking him to tell me what is really going on. The next time I talked to him, I was on my way to work, he did not bring the message up at all. I had to pressure him into giving me the truth. He finally told me he could not love me the way I needed or desired. He said I needed someone who could treat me good. He just didn't have those romantic feelings for me anymore. He couldn't manufacture those past feelings and wanted to be casual friends. After he said this, I got off the phone immediately because I could not talk to him at that moment. I cried with a friend while driving to work. Eventually, I called my mom and she informed me it was good he told me before I moved there. She had a great point, but at this moment, I still loved him and wanted to be with him. She also reminded me I had a lot of faith and strength, and I would be ok. Then I called into work because there was no way I could work in this state. I was devastated. I had so many emotions going on. The two friends I had talked to that night prayed for me and I needed that. I got some good rest that night and the next day I informed people we had broken up. Eventually, I had my final conversation with him because we didn't really go further with the conversation after he told me he didn't love me anymore. He said I was a good woman, but he thought we should be friends instead because he just didn't have those romantic feelings for me anymore. I wanted to know was it something that I did to make him not love me anymore, but he said I did nothing wrong. I felt he pulled a cowardly move by withholding this information for so long, but he apologized for hurting me then and throughout the relationship. He wished me the best in my business and prayed that my heart heals soon and that I find someone that loves me the way I needed and desired.

This was the hardest breakup for me for so many reasons. We were together for a long time, I thought how we got connected was such a sweet story, I was preparing to be his wife if that was God's will, so my actions were of someone preparing to be a wife. I shared some very intimate things with him. I was working on aiming to love him the way God wanted us to love people and he was attached to so many aspects of my business. I felt like we didn't have a real chance with us being long distance, so I wanted to try the relationship between us in the same city before it was called off. I gave so much of myself to please him and it still ended. I was finally dating a man that understood my values on premarital sex and he was a virgin which was why I was so upset as well. On top of the breakup, I was trying to grow my business while only working part-time. I wasn't sure what direction I needed to go since our relationship ended. After the breakup, I felt betrayed, unloved, hopeless, and unwanted. I also felt defeated because I tried so hard to fix the relationship and that was out of my control. I was ashamed because I was excited to tell people I was moving to where he was, and a lot of my business content was about him and our relationship as we walked the celibacy journey. Believe it or not I was hoping to reunite. I had a fear of being married or loving again because I didn't want to take the chance of experiencing this type of hurt again or something worse. I knew he wasn't perfect, but I didn't expect what had come from him. He was trying to do the right thing, but he still lived a lie for a while and that hurt. I felt stupid to tell people I stayed with him for four years and didn't get an engagement ring even though I wanted to move before I decided if I wanted to spend the rest of my life with him. Nobody would probably understand my rationale for staying that long. I felt cheated because I did the right thing by finding a good guy that truly loves God, respects my values, and was stable. I wasn't desperate to be married and was busy walking in my purpose, and I did my best to live a Christian lifestyle, so I felt let down by God. I just didn't feel like I could trust another man after this experience. To be honest I wanted him to hurt like I was hurting. I mean how could he lie like that for so long and not feel guilty or did he? But I knew I had to get my heart right about him, God (I was mad at God too), and the relationship if I wanted to please God, be happy, and move on with my life. He was wrong and so was I because I ignored what God was showing me, so I had to forgive myself and him. I understood him wanting to wait to see if his feelings would change and not wanting to hurt my feelings, but that was a long time to wait it out without having a plan to do something different in the relationship. This was the worst pain ever. I would have rather been dead than to feel this pain. Now I understood better why people would want to hurt themselves to relieve emotional pain. I would cry in the bathroom at work, around the house, in the car, before I went to sleep, and at church. I cried pretty much everywhere lol. I wanted to stop going to my church because it reminded me of him. I would relive the breakup and our relationship repeatedly which caused headaches and chest pains. I had such a strong tie to him it felt like I had died when he left. I had several pity parties for about a month. I felt so lost and exhausted because for the last year I had put so much energy into the relationship and trying to move. So, I wasn't sure what my next move was supposed to be. I did, however, feel relieved because I felt free to be more of myself, to get back to some goals I wanted to accomplish before I got married, and I didn't have to deal with the things I didn't like about him from the beginning.

I knew healing from this breakup would have to be big due to the length of the relationship and what he meant to me. The first thing I knew I would do is go on a fast. A fast is abstaining from food and spending that extra time with God. I usually fasted once a week, but for this breakup, I needed to do something different. I did a partial fast for two weeks. So, I started the fast on June 15 because that was the day my ex and I started talking and getting to know each other, and I wanted to create a new memory. I asked God to make this day different and special for me. After I spent time with God that morning, I took myself to the movies and I had an amazing time! During the fast and the rest of the healing process in 2018, I learned more about healing, the love of God, and self-worth in Christ through the Bible, Bible plans, books, YouTube, podcasts, and music. I also recited some confessions about moving on, the love of God, and self-esteem. I thought I was cool with my self-esteem until this break up happened. I also wrote in my journal. I was so broken that I was desperate for God and nothing else mattered but God at this moment. I also took a break from my business and social media. I needed more time with God because I needed direction now that my plans had changed. During my fast, I was reminded that Jesus was sent to heal the brokenhearted, so I had to take advantage of that. Of course, I cried a lot (mainly in the first and 2nd month) and I would even have fantasies about my ex during the process. I texted him about two weeks later because I was just so angry and wanted even more answers. That was not a good idea. It made me even more angry and sad. He confirmed there wasn't another woman and he wasn't dating anyone after we broke up. I remember telling people not to send me anything about dating and marriage because I just wanted to focus on the love of God. There was an emotional soul tie that needed to be broken. A soul tie is a cleaving together, a relationship whereby two souls are joined or knitted together, and in a sense become as one. Soul ties that exist on an emotional level are based on emotional attachments such as common feelings of love, fear or hatred. When there is not an even balance, healthy soul ties can become distorted perverted. (Banks, 16-19) Therefore, I had to break the tie with a prayer. I also signed up for therapy to help me heal. I had never seen a therapist, but I knew for this breakup I would need all the help I could get. I needed one on one attention from a professional to help me process everything without being judgmental. Therefore, I asked a friend/therapist to recommend a male Christian therapist. I was able to get eight free sessions with him through my job. I removed my ex from my social media accounts and my phone. I got rid of things such as jewelry, letters, and pictures. About a month and a half later I no longer felt shocked by the reason we broke up. I had accepted it even though it still hurt. During the healing process, I also felt alone initially. It felt like I was alone in how I felt about the breakup and that other women were not transparent about how they felt or healed after one. When I started working on this book, I talked to other women and read about grief in a book about healing from a breakup, I got a chance to see that I was not crazy for how I was feeling or acting. After about a month or so, I finally asked my dad for his thoughts on the situation. He let me know that I have a lot going for myself and that the distance probably affected my ex's feelings about me. I heard another man give me similar feedback. That gave me even more closure because I then had a better understanding of how men think. Even without this feedback, I still needed to be confident in myself even if someone leaves me because they didn't love me. Besides therapy, I went to deliverance sessions at my church for about 2 ½ months. We covered unforgiveness, pride, rebellion, and so much more. During these sessions, I realized I had hurt him also when I broke up with him at the beginning of our relationship, but we immediately got back together because I wanted to. I emailed him my apology. I expected little feedback, but boy was I surprised. He accepted my apology and apologized again for hurting me. He also once again wished me the best in business, finding a husband and building a family soon. That last part made me regret sending the email. I screamed in my mind that that was supposed to be you!!! The hurt I experienced after the breakup all came back. I told myself, man, I'm going deeper in my study of the love of God, and my mission is to help as many girls and ladies as I can now so that they could avoid some of what I experienced. I also attended a couple of special events at churches such as concerts and revivals which strengthened me to go on. Even though I was hurting, sometimes, I said a prayer for him just as I did when we were dating. It was hard, but deep down inside, I didn't want his life to be over because of what happened between us. I finally stopped reliving the relationship and breakup repeatedly after about two months. About three months after my breakup in September, I was ready to get back to setting career goals, so I started job searching. This was so exciting for me because I knew I was getting back to things being more stable. As my birthday came in this month, I prayed that I would not have a horrible birthday. It was the complete opposite! It was more than I asked for! I won't lie, I missed my ex, but I enjoyed my birthday more than I missed him. He emailed me a happy birthday, but I wished he hadn't. Now I don't know how I would have felt if he didn't. Oh well, I needed to stop dwelling on what ifs. I just simply said thank you to him. In October, I decided to finally get rid of the rest of the gifts, pictures, and emails about him. It felt like a death all over again but I was ready to stop loving him so I wouldn't feel the pain anymore. During this month, I even read my book again and learned something new about my behavior patterns in romantic relationships. My first boyfriend got distant the second time around we dated, and I chased after him to get some answers, but nothing was really established. In November, I completed all my therapy sessions. Therapy had to be one of the best decisions I made in my life! The advice from family and friends was nice but I needed to process this breakup with someone trained in handling this type of situation and didn't know me or my ex. One of my coworkers could tell the counseling helped me because I looked happy and free. I didn't know she was paying attention but that was good to hear. Before the sessions started, I prayed that God would speak through the therapist. In therapy, I was able to get to the root of why I was so hurt by the breakup. It was because of the spirit of rejection. I am not an expert on it but, I recognized the fruit of it in my life due to learning about it in church and self-study. The fruit of it was revealed after several therapy sessions. Being insecure about oneself and performing to be accepted are some ways it shows up in your life. (Eckhardt, 45, 124). I had no problem with being alone, but I was performing to be accepted in this relationship, and I felt a lot of insecurity towards the end. I also based my identity off what people thought of me or what I did instead of basing my identity off of what God says about me. I thought about the events that happened in my life that could have brought about the spirit of rejection. I knew this time I was going to have to deal with the spirit of rejection so I can move on with my life. I reread *Destroying the Spirit of Rejection: Receive Love and Acceptance and Find Healing* by John Eckhardt. This time I read and discussed it with a friend because I can heal from things better if I can talk about it. As of the end of 2018, I was still reading the book. During therapy, we focused a lot on building my self-esteem, seeing both sides of the breakup, and how to move forward. I got new revelations of scriptures I had heard a thousand times. Romans 8:28 ([28] And we know that God causes everything to work together[a] for the good of those who love God and are called according to his purpose for them) is a scripture I had read repeatedly but the way the therapist broke it down resonated with me. The word everything in the scripture includes the good and bad times. When the bad happens to us, we forget that God will use that and the good that happens for His purpose for our lives. So even though this breakup shook my world, He would use it for an amazing purpose. That makes me hopeful about the future. The therapist's final advice for me for the rest of my healing process was to work on my self-esteem. Also, in November, I finally accepted the emotions that will come from Thanksgiving and Christmas and not being with my ex. The last time we saw each other was Christmas 2017. That was the first time I spent Christmas away from my family and the last day of that trip was sad. So, as I saw Christmas festivities and décor come up, I thought about that and it made me sad, hurt, and angry. In the meantime, I received amazing news on December 5, 2018!

This day had marked six months since our breakup. One of the goals that I wanted to accomplish by the end of 2018 was to get a new job, and that is exactly what happened! I was overjoyed because I needed this new start. This job fell in line with what I was looking for as far as responsibilities. I was seeing more light at the end of the tunnel. I was so looking forward to starting this job and getting back on track financially and emotionally! Christmas and the end of the year were extremely hard due to memories of us. I peeked on his social media accounts just to see if anything was posted about him or a new girlfriend. I saw nothing. I don't plan on doing that again lol. I trusted God to get me through the holiday season and He did. But I was so glad that the year was over. I knew 2019 would be totally different for me. I am not completely healed but I have come a long way since June 2018. For the rest of my healing process, I will continue to study about self-worth in Christ, unforgiveness, and whatever else God brings to my attention. I didn't know I was so broken, but I am looking forward to my day of complete healing.

Even though this breakup was a painful experience, I am grateful for it because it allowed me to learn more about the love of God and my self-worth in Christ. I feel free to be me because I kind of lost myself in this relationship, and I noticed areas of my life that still need improvement before I enter a marriage. I am also learning how to truly be still and wait on God for direction for every moment of my life. I was also excited to get back to doing things I wanted to do before marriage such as traveling, becoming more independent and getting rid of debt. The breakup also gave me new content for my business. I am not ready to get back in a relationship and get married, but I have hope in God he will bring the right man for me when it's time. I know that God will bring me a man that will be honored to have me as his wife once I allow Him to complete the work He has to do in me. If I thought my ex was the jackpot, I know the real man for me will be completely amazing! I sowed so much good in this relationship, I am looking forward to reaping what I sowed!

My Breakup Tips:

Please study the love of God for yourself. Understand who you are in Christ before getting into the next relationship. Be patient in the healing process, even though it sucks, it is necessary to walk through it and you can learn a lot during it. Don't compare your healing process with someone else's. Every person and situation is different, but the same God heals us all. No matter how bad the situation was or is, God still has a bright future for you. He had a plan for your life before you even came into the world.

Chapter 2

Valencia

My most difficult breakup was with a college sweetheart introduced through a mutual acquaintance. We dated the following semester in January. Three days before Valentine's Day his high school sweetheart told him they had a son together. He wanted to do the right thing, so we broke up. This breakup was difficult for me because he basically acted like I didn't exist, yet always wanted to know where I was or what I was doing. For example, I went home for the weekend and he called me asking why I didn't tell him I was leaving campus. When I tried to contact him over the summer months because of some things we left unsaid, I never heard from him, but when he heard I was leaving the country, he showed up at my house. The mixed emotions and signals were too much for me. I was hurt because I felt like our relationship didn't have a real chance. It took a couple of months for me to heal. I started the healing process by talking with my mom about what was going on, and she showed me how to make myself less available and accessible. It was about four months before I was healed. I knew I was healed when he called me out of the blue and I ignored the calls. What helped me heal from this breakup the most was taking the advice of not being so accessible. Surprisingly, we ended up getting back together, getting married, and having kids! We've been married for 13 years. From our relationship and the healing process, I learned that I needed to discover things from previous relationships before starting a relationship with someone and that I can't take what's said at face value.

Valencia's

Breakup Tip:

Take your time and don't be as available and accessible as you were before

Chapter 3

Alisa

My most difficult breakup was with a live-in boyfriend. He came home from work one day and told me he would not be coming home from work tomorrow. I asked him if he was going somewhere after work tomorrow. He told me that when he left that morning, he would be taking his belongings and not coming back. This was a difficult breakup because I was unaware that he was cheating on me. I felt angry, hurt, unwanted and unloved. It took a year to move on but about five years to completely heal. I did not understand that I had allowed that experience to create trust issues. To help me heal, I read several books which included a few daily devotionals by Joyce Meyers. I talked with close relatives and friends. It felt like I was healing when I returned to my normal routine, my smile came back, and my heart felt the urge to love again. I knew I was healed when I had peace in my heart and peace of mind. Being 100% truthful about the role I played in that relationship helped me heal the most. My healing process allowed me to learn how to love myself and others unconditionally. I also learned how to forgive even when I don't want to. I learned how to look at the facts of a situation and realize that I may have to accept it for what it truly is.

Alisa's

Breakup Tip:

Do not allow your past experiences to stop you from loving again. Be open and honest with yourself about how you feel and then push past the fears, tears, hurt and anger so you can rediscover the love within.

Alisa is currently dating

Chapter 4

Victoria

My worst break up was with a man that I felt like I was meant to be with because he gave me everything I wanted and needed. Things started off perfect but then we started having issues. It was both of us, but he only saw my issues. I was very codependent and had low self-esteem. He never failed to let me know how beautiful I was and that's what kept me holding on because I never had that with anyone else. There were so many red flags I never saw because I was blind to it all. He reminded me of my dad, and I was like my mom in our relationship. I put up with emotional abuse and disrespect until he left me and that's when God came into my life. This breakup hurt the most because he was like my father and that's all that I knew. After the breakup, I wanted to die. I literally felt my heart breaking. I took one year to heal from that breakup. In order to heal from it, I kept myself busy. I joined a women's bible study, went to church on weekdays, joined a beauty for ashes class, started Christian therapy, and looked for accountability partners who were going through the same thing. I felt like I was healing within six months of my beauty for ashes class. I knew I was healed when I saw a picture of him with another woman and my heart didn't drop. I was happy he was following God and had a good woman beside him. What helped me heal the most was my beauty for ashes class and the Lord. I am thankful for the breakup and healing process because it allowed me to be free!!!

Victoria's Breakup Tip

Stay single and heal completely.
Let God in and let him be your husband
and allow him to fill that void!

Victoria is not dating at this time

Chapter 5

Joy

My worst breakup was from a two-year on and off relationship that ended when he moved away and stopped contacting me. It felt as if someone had died. It sent me into a depression that was resolved with counseling and support from friends and family. I took this breakup the hardest because there was no reason or closure. I felt broken, lost, and hopeless. I took about six months to heal from the breakup. During the first few months after the breakup, I thought I could handle it. When I noticed I was avoiding friends and activities I knew it was more than I could handle alone. I went to my doctor and she offered me a prescription to help "get me over the hump," but I didn't want meds. So, she referred me to a counselor where there were lots of open and honest discussions. It allowed me to deal with some unconfronted past grief and loss. I wrote letters to the person hurting me with no intention of them reading them. I forced myself to spend time with friends. A book and video on healing helped me a lot. For the nights I couldn't sleep I'd just play the video over and over. I started to feel like healing was taking place when I realized why I was holding on. I had experienced so much loss that was out of my control that I was holding on so tight to this relationship trying to control it. I was completely healed when I was no longer angry. I could hear his name and not sob. Going out with friends and actually enjoying myself instead of being held captive by my own thoughts was a sign of healing as well. What helped me to heal the most was discovering myself, dealing with past emotions, and knowing that I was grieving and that not everyone grieves the same way. Last, realizing that I was holding onto something that was never there to begin with helped me heal the most. The breakup and healing process allowed me to realize that I can't control everything and that is perfectly ok. I can't choose how people love me, but I can choose how I love myself and how I love them.

Joy's

Breakup Tip:

Take the time to heal and learn something new about yourself. Sometimes we lose a piece of ourselves in relationships, and we must put the pieces back together before we can give our hearts away.

Joy is currently dating

Chapter 6

Faith

My worst breakup came from what seemed to be a safe and comfortable relationship. He was very respectful, treated me well, got along with my family and friends and had a lot of the same hobbies as I did. However, it later turned into something toxic at times. His jealousy turned into paranoia, and he became less interested in a more serious commitment. We got to where we were breaking up every few months. Sometimes, we would have no contact at all. Then, we'd get back together and everything would be great, initially, before we fell back into the same pattern that led to previous breakups. The final breakup came after I felt God instructing me to completely close that chapter of my life so I could move on to what He had for me. This was the hardest breakup for me because I considered it my most serious relationship, despite the down times. During the 10 years we were off and on, we appreciated each other's family and friends, shared property, and traveled the world. It was hard to lose all of that, and I thought I gave someone the best years of my life. The hardest part of it all was I lost my father during this relationship and it just killed me to think the man I married would not know my father. That kept me there quite a bit longer than anything else. After the breakup, I felt lonely and frustrated but hopeful and liberated. I left a dark situation and I knew that relationship had never been what I really wanted. I had just settled into what seemed like a "makes sense" relationship. I knew God had better in store for me. I took one year to heal. I didn't date or get into a relationship during this time. I was praying hard for "the one" but I was letting God take me through a process. To help heal from this breakup, I developed a closer relationship with God. He had my companion waiting but I needed to work on myself before I could get there. I needed to disconnect from what I had been living for years with my ex. At times, the relationship had made me question my worth and other things. That year brought healing, re-direction, a closer relationship and dependency on God. I spent more time with family and friends and kind of found myself and my joy again. It was a few months before I felt free of the effects the relationship had on me. I knew I was healed because I felt free and I had no more bitterness about losing a lot of time. God helped me heal the most from this breakup. The breakup allowed me to learn to never lose focus on God. God is the only one that can make me whole. As long as I know that and He is my priority and the center of my relationship, it will all work out. I am also stronger and more valuable than I may have let myself believe.

Faith's

Breakup Tip:

It is okay to focus on YOU - to take time to love yourself back to being healthy and free. And it is okay to be picky! Know what you want, know what you're worth and never settle for less.

Faith is currently married

Chapter 7

Talitha

In 2003, I met a guy on Yahoo, and we met in person after a few telephone conversations. We met at his house, and that was a mistake. I was only 17, and I thought he was 24. When I turned 18 the next month, he took me club hopping for the first time and bought me a few mixed drinks. He convinced me to sleep with him early into the relationship. Later I found out he was really 31. I also found out that he was only renting a bedroom instead of owning the house. The business he owned was a joke and his only income was a disability check. I dated him for about another month and let him meet my family and even brought him to church. He proposed to me with a $50 pawn shop ring he was going to make weekly payments on. The cost didn't matter but based on that he would never be able to take care of me and a family. After 3 months into the relationship, things got twisted. He moved into an off-campus dormitory at a local university based on a counterfeit college acceptance letter and fake schedule he stole from a student he had been sleeping with behind my back. In fact, he was sleeping with several girls on campus. He hacked into their phones, including mine, and sent ugly threatening messages to all of us from each other's phone to make us hate each other and fight over him. He even lied saying he was purposely infecting us with STDs. If that were true, I'm so glad I wasn't affected. My dad and crazy cousins got involved and scared this guy so badly he literally ran for his life, and that was the end of our relationship. I took this break up hard because I was young. It was my first time dealing with a grown man and I didn't listen to those who tried to warn me. As a result, I went through hell. After the breakup, I felt empty, ashamed, lonely and scared this guy had given me an STD. Waiting on test results made me physically ill, but they came out negative. I prayed to God like never before, and I turned my life around to live a Christian lifestyle from that day forward. It took about two months to heal, but another 12 years to not feel scarred by the situation. It was like post-traumatic stress disorder. The thought and sight of him would bring me to an anxiety attack. To start the healing process, I turned to God. I felt like healing was taking place after I forgave myself and let go of guilt and shame. The post-traumatic stress disorder melted away when I realized he had no power over me. Initial healing felt like a fresh start. I could laugh and enjoy life again. I knew I was healed because I stopped running and hiding from him. He continued to stalk me and my family through social media. It was a lot of work trying to keep up with all of his accounts and blocking them, but one day I just stopped. There's no chase if I stop running. And that's what he wanted, to have power over me through fear. Like when Forest Gump just stopped running. I just stopped. And so did he. My faith helped me heal the most from the breakup.

Talitha's

Breakup Tip:

Learn from your mistakes, but don't beat yourself up. Allow yourself to be sad and angry, but never hold hatred. Try to give yourself less and less time each day to dwell on the breakup. Set a cry it out timer, even, until you're down from maybe two hours a day to five minutes.

Talitha is currently married

Chapter 8

Briana

My worst breakup was from a relationship I knew I had no business being in. Everything seemed to go great; however, my spirit was never at peace. We even talked about getting married. When I started reconnecting with God, I could not continue to play both sides of the fence. It was the hardest thing I had to do because I loved this person and knew I was causing them a lot of pain and I would be hated because of this decision. After the breakup I felt like I was hated, borderline depressed, hurt in my soul and I felt guilty for causing this person pain. It took about two years to heal. To heal I had to cut all ties with the person, spend a lot of time pursuing my relationship with God through prayer and seeking Him, learn to be by myself to learn who I really was, and participate in deliverance. I was healing when God showed me the truth about the relationship. He began to show me areas where my ex showed signs of not really loving me but manipulating and taking advantage of me. Then God began to show me myself and how I ended up in the relationship and how it was harmful. I knew I was healed when I went from being sad, depressed, guilty and angry because I had to end it, to being grateful that I was set free from it. It was liberating and made me want to help others. I had more confidence and love for myself. I was gaining healthy self-esteem and finding myself falling in love with God and really enjoying life and family. Trusting God's plan and being honest with God about how I was feeling, being open to change, and cutting all ties helped me heal the most. The breakup and healing process taught me so much! It taught me the following:

- Never allow a person to fill a God-sized void
- I was stronger than I thought
- God takes the sting away when you intimately get involved with Him and walk in obedience
- Healing is done in layers and may not happen all at once
- There are is strength and growth in healing

- Detoxification is necessary
- You can easily lose yourself and your moral compass by getting involved in the wrong relationships
- Be mindful of what you "feel" you need because it can be the very time Satan needs to keep you hooked in the wrong relationship,
- Be whole first
- Set clear boundaries
- Never be afraid to lose someone
- Don’t lose yourself in the process.

Briana's

Breakup Tip:

Go at God's pace and don't be afraid to embrace the mirror when God shows it to you, it's truly the key to receiving the healing you need

Briana is currently married

Chapter 9

Hope

My most difficult break up was from my first divorce. This breakup was difficult because I believed that the covenant would hold us together for life. After the breakup, I felt like I wanted to die. I cried myself to sleep and questioned my own worth. I took over five years to heal. Instead of trying to heal from the breakup, I started dating to cover my pain. I got pregnant five years later and married again. That lasted 10 years, and then I began the healing process for both of my divorces. I felt like I was healing once I placed God as the head of my life 15 years after that breakup. During this time, I also had three children. To heal from the breakup, I took one year of not dating and focused on God. I took advantage of every sermon, every bible study, had quiet time, read books about being whole, and one day I began to truly love myself. I knew then, that I was restored and whole. Chasing after God and feeding myself the word every day instead of just on Sundays helped me heal the most. The breakup and healing process taught me it is my own responsibility to love me, no one else can love me like I love me, and it's a bonus when someone else notices how amazing I am. I am amazing whether or not he knows it.

Hope's

Breakup Tip:

Turn to God and put him back in FIRST PLACE. Give yourself time alone between relationships to heal. You cannot heal from your past relationship by getting under someone else.

Hope is currently dating

Scriptures and Affirmations

These are some scriptures and affirmations that helped me during the healing process.

I like to write them out on index cards or save them in my Bible app and recite them daily. There were some I posted in my room where I could see them daily. Some of my affirmations I came up with on my own, and the rest came from the Bible. I would definitely get a lot of them from the Bible because God created us and He already knows us. As you spend time in God's word and read or listen to things to help you heal, you will find so much more like I did! However, these will get you started.

Scriptures

1. Jeremiah 29:11
2. Zephaniah 3:17
3. Psalms 147:3
4. Luke 4:18
5. Psalms 27:13-14
6. Isaiah 43:18-19
7. I John 2:19
8. Psalms 34:18
9. Psalms 51:17
10. Philippians 3:14
11. Psalms 118:17
12. Psalms 34:17
13. Isaiah 43:4
14. Isaiah 49:16
15. Jeremiah 31:3

Self-Affirmations

Write your own because God made you unique!

1. I am more than good enough.

2. I am loved by God.

3. I am accepted by God.

4. I am a joy to be around.

5. I am one of a kind.

6. I am a masterpiece.

7. God wants me.

8. I am a beautiful woman with good sense.

9. I am courageous.

10. I am a good woman.

Suggested Books to Read

These are books I have used during the healing process so far.

1. *Woman Thou Art Loosed* by TD Jakes
2. *Destroying the Spirit of Rejection: Receive Love and Acceptance and Find Healing* by John Eckhardt
3. *The Lady, Her Lover, Her Lord* by TD Jakes
4. *Armor of God* by Priscilla Shirer
5. *Breaking Unhealthy Soul Ties* by Bill and Sue Banks

References

Banks, William D., and Sue Banks. *Breaking Unhealthy Soul-Ties: Do Your Relationships Produce Bondage or Joy?* Impact Christian Books, 1999.

Eckhardt, John. *Destroying the Spirit of Rejection.* Charisma House, 2016.

Connect with Breaking it Down with C Jackson!

Web: www.breakingitdowncj.com

Facebook: Breaking it Down with C Jackson

Instagram: @breakingitdowncj

Twitter: @BreakingJackson

Youtube: Breaking it Down with C Jackson

Made in the USA
Columbia, SC
06 March 2023

13298277R00041